Katie Clemons

LET'S CELEBRATE YOUR STORY

Mother AND Daughter TOGETHER

A shared journal for teen girls & their moms

sourcebooks
eXplore

To Amelia and Charlotte

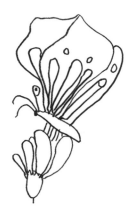

Drawings by Niklas (age 8)
and Linden (age 4)

Copyright © 2023 by Katie Clemons LLC
Cover and internal design © 2023 by Sourcebooks
Cover and internal design by Amanda Mustard
Illustrations by Amanda Mustard

Sourcebooks and the colophon are registered trademarks of Sourcebooks.

Published by Sourcebooks eXplore, an imprint of Sourcebooks Kids

P.O. Box 4410, Naperville, Illinois 60567–4410
(630) 961-3900
sourcebookskids.com

Source of Production: PrintPlus Limited, Shenzhen,
Guangdong Province, China
Date of Production: March 2023
Run Number: 5030197

Printed and bound in China.
PP 10 9 8 7 6 5 4 3 2 1

Growing inside

I'd like to tell you that I was a perfectly confident teenager as my mom and I pulled into the high school parking lot that August morning. She drove a minivan. I had a new bag, trendy bangs, and adorable shoes. But I also had doubts that I thought she didn't know.

"You're going to have a good day, Katie," she said, as she looked at me through the rearview mirror.

"Sure, Mom."

I'd seen too many TV shows to believe her. While my middle school classmates had probably all blossomed into these incredibly cool high schoolers over summer break, I couldn't even talk the teen talk yet. My body was changing in weird ways. My emotions rollercoastered without my control. I felt panicked about my future and desperate for approval. I was awkward and scared out of my mind.

While I unbuckled my seatbelt, my mom turned around in her seat. I swear she could sense my anxiety—the way only a mom can notice. "You're going to have a good day," she said again. "You just have to see it that way."

These days, with the hectic schedules our families juggle, I know it's often tricky to find the right circumstances for open dialogue or for a mom to understand her daughter's changing needs. Yet sometimes, a girl just needs her mom to advocate for her and love her exactly as she is.

A teenage girl is a lot like a caterpillar that's built a chrysalis around herself as she grows out of childhood. Someone might look at it and think nothing is going on, but big changes are happening inside. One day, a beautiful butterfly will hatch, spread its wings, and take flight.

Now that I'm a mom, I understand that a butterfly only hatches on its own. I also know how difficult it must have been for my mom to drive away whenever she saw me struggling. When my child wrestles with uncertainty, my primal reaction is to reach for her hand so we can tackle the world together. I get so wrapped up in my need to nurture that I forget: sometimes my child needs to find her way without me.

Looking back, I still remember when school ended that day. I swung my bag over my shoulder and walked to where my mom was waiting with the minivan.

"How was the first day of school?" she asked as I climbed in.

"Oh, you know," I shrugged. "It wasn't so bad."

She raised her eyebrows. I raised mine. Then we both burst into laughter.

"Okay," I said. "Parts of it were fantastic! Though some parts weren't as good..."

"But you did it!" she cheered. "Let's go home. You can tell me about it."

Mother-daughter moments like these are threads that connect me forever with my mom's love.

Keeping a journal together can also help both you and your mom become more aware of yourselves and each other. Writing prompts strengthen your sense of compassion as you view the world through each other's unique lens of age and experience. Journaling together encourages you to slow down and really listen. It's a space where you can feel confident and comfortable being yourself. This journal is like a peek inside that chrysalis.

These five guideposts will help you get the most from your story-catching time together.

1. You make the rules.

Delve into this journal however it suits you and your mom and throw away every preconceived notion you've heard about journaling. Complete the pages sequentially or flutter from page to page as they strike the two of you. Jot down a little or a lot. Add or alter anything. If a prompt doesn't resonate with you, cross it out. Cover it up. Make up your own. Curl up on the couch and write together or pass the book back and forth in turn.

Your mom's stories go on pages that begin "Dear Mom" or "Mom Writes." Corresponding "Dear Daughter" and "Daughter Writes" pages are your opportunity to respond or launch different dialogue. When you see a "Dear Daughter" page, imagine your mom prompting you: "Hey your-name-here, I was wondering..." She's asking the question and awaiting your response below. Then intermixed throughout the book are spaces to doodle, write, and add keepsakes together. Photographs are completely optional.

2. Tell your true stories.

When we talk, it's easy to get caught up in fretting about what we perceive other people will think or say. Use this journal to focus on telling your own perspective and describing what you see and how you feel. Be you. Use your favorite expressions. Be honest about mistakes made and lessons learned. You do not need perfection.

I can compose run-on sentences that fill half a page whenever I journal. There's an abundance of exclamation marks and beverage stains from I don't know what. I'm certain I'll never be able to spell a single French word (bougie? bourgeois?). But you know what? I keep going. The best discoveries come from letting your pen wander across the page.

You just have to start.

3. Listen completely.

Try to understand what each other is really communicating. While you may feel tempted to get angry, point out faults, or lecture in these pages, remember that this journal is your opportunity to peek inside each other's heads and hearts so that you can see the world through each other's eyes. Does she feel misunderstood? Does she need help or crave connection?

Some entries in this journal address things you already know about each other. Many are just for fun. And then there are pages that spur memories from childhood. You may even discover emotions, perspectives, or entire stories you weren't aware of—from each other or yourselves. Respond immediately or give yourself time to reflect.

4. Enjoy!

Think of this journal as a place to play together. Jot "love ya" all you want. Draw stick figures or sketch. Experiment with every marker and pen you can find. Underline words or color them in. Instead of dotting an i, give it a heart. Doodle mustaches, block letters, emojis, speech bubbles, and arrows. Embellish with stickers and mementos. Snap photos together and adhere them with glue or double-sided tape. Be as serious or silly as you want.

5. Go beyond this book.

Come to my website for more mother-daughter storycatching activities and projects. My family loves these Saturday self-care recommendations, adult coloring pages, and cheesy-sweet lunchbox notes. They're all free at:

katieclemons.com/a/d5JZ/

Thanks for letting this journal and me join your journey. Write to me any time **howdy@katieclemons.com** (I answer all my mail), or tag me on social media **@katierclemons #katieclemonsjournals #motheranddaughtertogether**.

You're going to have a good day. Get ready to spread your wings, and... Let's celebrate your story!

but **inner beauty** turns the heart.

–Helen J. Russell

Let's start here

Our full names are

_____

Mom

_____

Daughter

We usually call each other

_____

We are _____ and _____ years old, which are fabulous ages because

_____

_____

We always say these expressions

Here's a drawing or
photograph of you and me doing
something we love

Today, we begin our story!

Date _____

Our Journal Guidelines

which ☐ are ☐ are not to be strictly followed

1. **Our top focus(es) in this journal will be to**
    ☐ Express our honest thoughts
    ☐ Use perfect grammar
    ☐ Let go of perfection and enjoy the process together
    ☐ Write what we perceive each other wants to read
    ☐ Create a snapshot of our life right now
    ☐ _____

    Thoughts

    _____
    _____
    _____

2. **Why are we interested in journaling together?**

    _____
    _____
    _____

3. **How often would we like to write back and forth?**

    _____
    _____
    _____

4. What could we do if we need more space to write?

_____

_____

_____

5. Do we need to answer the prompts in numerical order?
   ☐ Yes ☐ No

6. How do we pass our journal back and forth? And how do we let each other know which page to turn to?

_____

_____

_____

7. Can anyone else look inside our journal or hear about what we're sharing?

_____

_____

_____

8. Are there any other guidelines we'd like to establish before we dive in?

_____

_____

_____

Daughter Writes

Mom, you make me smile when you

_____

_____

_____

_____

Here's you being so

_____!

And me grinning like a

_____!

Mom Writes

Daughter, you make me smile when you

_____

_____

_____

_____

Here's you being so
_____!

And me grinning like a
_____!

This is us!

We can sing every word of

Daughter _____

Mom _____

We are obsessed with

> Daughter

> Mom

We always wear

> Daughter

> Mom

We can't decide if

Daughter _____

Mom _____

We get stubborn about

Daughter _____

Mom _____

We're always laughing when

Daughter _____

Mom _____

We Write

We lose track of time when

Daughter _____

Mom _____

We're pretty good at

Daughter _____

Mom _____

We're really bad at

Daughter _____

Mom _____

Our most treasured possessions are

Daughter

Mom

We collect a lot of

Daughter

Mom

We want this journal to be filled with

Daughter _____

Mom _____

Daughter Writes

Little things I'm grateful for right now

1 _____

2 _____

3 _____

4 _____

5 _____

6 _____

7 _____

Daughter Writes

Mom Writes

Little things I'm grateful for right now

1 _____

2 _____

3 _____

4 _____

5 _____

6 _____

7 _____

Mom Writes

Dear Daughter,

Which school subject is your favorite? _____

Why do you enjoy it so much? _____

_____

_____

Why do you think other people struggle with it? _____

_____

_____

Tell me about something you're working on in this subject. _____

_____

_____

_____

_____

_____

Is there anything you'd like to learn more about? _____

_____

_____

How can I help you explore the topic more? _____

_____

_____

Daughter Writes

Dear Mom,

What are your thoughts on what I wrote about learning? _____

_____

_____

_____

_____

_____

_____

_____

_____

_____

_____

Tell me about a subject you loved when you were my age. _____

_____

_____

_____

_____

How does knowing that subject help your life today? _____

_____

_____

_____

_____

Mom Writes

This is our hair

At this very second!

Daughter   Mom

When it's looking fabulous

Daughter   Mom

On a no-good-very-bad hair day

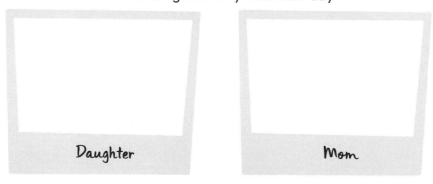

Daughter   Mom

We Write

Here's a picture of you and me with our entire family.

You know you're a part of our family if you

Say _____

Eat _____

Appreciate _____

Our theme song could be _____

We think our crew gets  stars.

Dear Mom,

What do you love about our family?

_____
_____
_____
_____

Is there anything that drives you crazy?

_____
_____
_____

Tell me a story about a time when you could see me being an important part of our family.

_____
_____
_____
_____
_____
_____
_____
_____
_____
_____
_____
_____

Mom Writes

Dear Daughter,

What do you love about our family?

_____

_____

_____

_____

Is there anything that embarrasses you or that you wish you could change?

_____

_____

_____

_____

How do you know we love you like crazy?

_____

_____

_____

_____

Tell me about a time when you felt proud to be a part of this family.

_____

_____

_____

_____

Daughter Writes

Mom Writes

One of the best gifts I ever received from you

(P.S. A gift isn't always a thing. Sometimes it's a gesture or words.)

Daughter Writes

One of the best gifts I ever received from you

Dear Mom,

What's your advice for when life gets hard?

Mom Writes

The greatest inside jokes and stories ever

Date

Dear Daughter,

What would you like to do this summer?

Daughter Writes

Dear Mom,

How did you spend the summers when you were my age?

Mom Writes

Daughter Writes

Here's what I did last Saturday

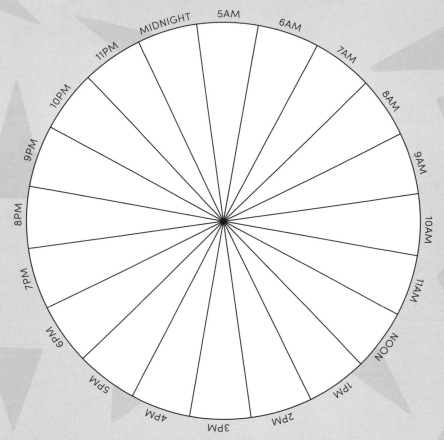

It was a typical / out-of-the-ordinary weekend day because

_____

_____

My day was 👍 👎 because _____

_____

Mom Writes

Here's what I did last Saturday

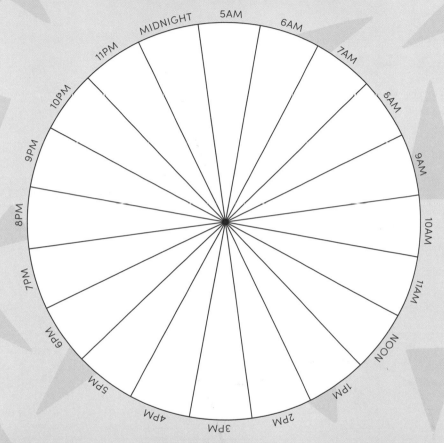

It was a typical / out-of-the-ordinary weekend day because

_____

_____

My day was 👍 👎 because _____

_____

You and Me

Beautiful and brave things we see women doing around us:

We Write

Dear Mom,

Tell me about the first time you held me.

Dear Daughter,

Do you ever feel like you have to hide your true self?

Why do you think you do that?

What could happen if you were completely yourself instead?

Daughter Writes

Dear Mom,

What do you think about what I wrote?

Do you ever hide who you really are?

Mom Writes

Daughter Writes

Mom, when things seem tough, always remember

Mom Writes

Daughter, when things seem tough, always remember

We Write

This movie or TV quote is such a good one.

Daughter Writes

It's so

Mom Writes

It's so

We Write

39

This is us road tripping!

If we jumped into a car for an impromptu vacation, we'd head to
_____.

You and Me

We'd bring _____
_____.

We'd snack on _____.
We'd drink _____.

We'd listen to _____.

We'd stop at

We Write

We'd sleep at _____

until _____ o'clock every morning.

We'd probably forget _____.

We'd laugh about _____
_____.

We'd have to buy _____.
_____.

Mom,
I'd ask you about

Daughter,
I'd ask you about

Daughter Writes

Here's something this week that

Went well

Challenged me

Irritated me

Cracked me up

Gave me stress or anxiety

Made me feel loved

Mom Writes

Here's something this week that

Went well

Challenged me

Irritated me

Cracked me up

Gave me stress or anxiety

Made me feel loved

Right now on our nightstands

Daughter Writes

Mom Writes

We Write

Daughter Writes

Mom, you deserve an award for

I'm proud to be your daughter because

_____

_____

_____

_____

_____

_____

_____

_____

Mom Writes

This or that?

circle each preference

Silver	Gold
Shower	Bath
Rich	Famous
Neutrals	Colors
Hair up	Hair down
Lipstick	Lip balm
Big house	Big trip
Influencer	Celebrity
City	Country
Flats	Heels
Jeans	Skirt/Dress
Shower gel	Soap bar
Roller coaster	Bumper cars
Security	Freedom
Book smarts	Street smarts
Football	Baseball

Daughter Writes

This or that?

Silver	Gold
Shower	Bath
Rich	Famous
Neutrals	Colors
Hair up	Hair down
Lipstick	Lip balm
Big house	Big trip
Influencer	Celebrity
City	Country
Flats	Heels
Jeans	Skirt/Dress
Shower gel	Soap bar
Roller coaster	Bumper cars
Security	Freedom
Book smarts	Street smarts
Football	Baseball

include any interesting asides!

lives IN it doesn't show up else.

—Steve Goodier

Dear Daughter,

How do you believe girls and women deserve to be treated?

Do you ever see people doing something different? How do you feel about that?

Do you think there are ways our society should change?

Daughter Writes

Dear Mom,

What are your thoughts on what I wrote?

How do you believe girls and women deserve to be treated?

Do you ever see people doing something different? How do you feel about that?

Has our society changed since you were my age? Do you think there are ways our society should change?

Mom Writes

Daughter Writes

One day, I'd like to

Try

Make

Learn

Visit

Speak

Understand

Enjoy

Love

Change

Help

Eat

Finish

Daughter Writes

Dear Mom,

Do you have any thoughts about what's on my list?

Which item surprised you?

Which one did you know I'd include?

Would you like to do any of them with me?

Dear Daughter,

What's something that you really enjoy creating?

Tell me about your process and inspiration.

How did you get interested in it?

Is there anything I could do to help you pursue it more?

Dear Mom,

What do you think about what I'm working on?

What's something that you really enjoy creating?

Tell me about your process and inspiration.

How did you get interested in it?

Dear Daughter,

Tell me about someone that you admire.

What's the number one reason this person inspires you so much?

How would you like to model this person as you grow?

Describe how our community or world is a better place because of this person.

Daughter Writes

Dear Mom,

What are your thoughts on what I wrote about someone I admire?

Do you see any traits in me that are similar to this person?

Tell me about someone you admire and the impact they've had.

We're totally capable of

Daughter

1 _____

2 _____

3 _____

4 _____

5 _____

6 _____

Mom

1 _____

2 _____

3 _____

4 _____

5 _____

6 _____

Date

Here's a page of different doodles and designs.

Mom Writes

Daughter, I'm so proud of you for

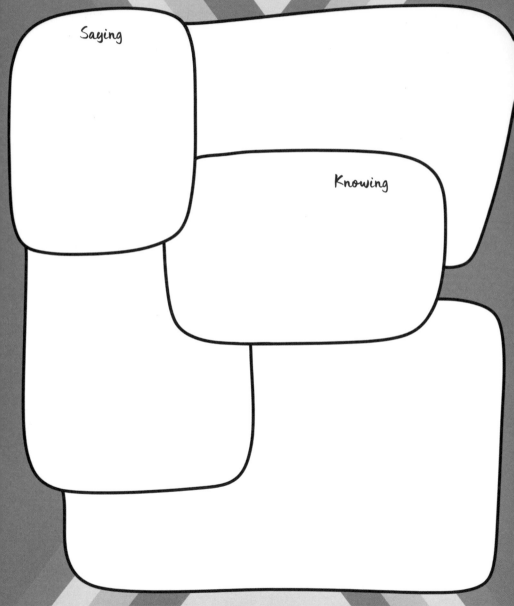

Saying

Knowing

Doing

Trying

Becoming

Daughter Writes

Mom, I admire how you're

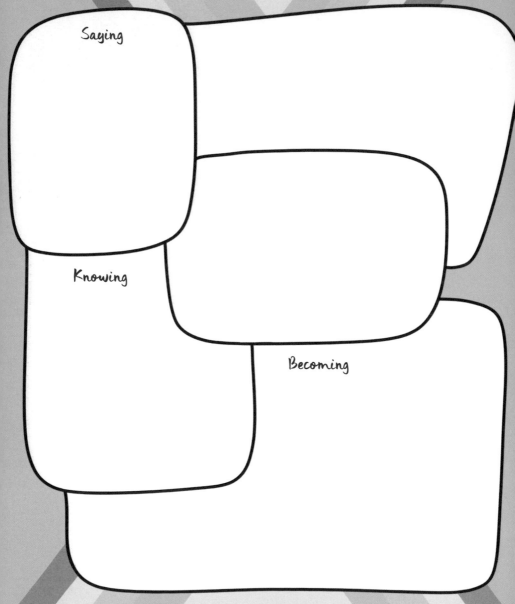

Saying

Knowing

Becoming

Doing

Trying

Dear Mom,

Tell me a story or two about when I was younger.

Mom Writes

Date

This is us

Opening an email from _____

Daughter	Mom

Learning that we just _____

Daughter	Mom

Cheering for _____

Daughter	Mom

We Write

65

Daughter Writes

If I had a **$1000 GIFT CARD** to shop at _____ , I'd get

Daughter Writes

Mom Writes

If I had a **$1000 GIFT CARD** to shop at _____ , I'd get

Daughter Writes

If I knew I could never fail, I would

Mom Writes

Daughter, here's what I know about
following your dreams.

Mom Writes

One day, I'd like to

Try

Make

Learn

Visit

Speak

Understand

Enjoy

Love

Change

Help

Eat

Finish

Dear Daughter,

Do you have any thoughts about what's on my list?

Which item surprised you?

Which one did you know I'd include?

Would you like to do any of them with me?

Daughter Writes

Daughter Writes

A playlist of songs I love

1 _____
_____

2 _____
_____

3 _____
_____

4 _____
_____

5 _____
_____

6 _____
_____

I enjoy listening to these songs while

I listen to music with this device _____

Here's where I set the volume

VOLUME

0   10

My signature
dance move

Mom Writes

A playlist of songs I love

1 _____

2 _____

3 _____

4 _____

5 _____

6 _____

I enjoy listening to these songs while

I listen to music with this device _____

Here's where I set the volume

VOLUME

0   10

My signature
dance move

Dear Daughter,

Tell me about your closest friends.

_____

_____

_____

What do you like doing with them?

_____

_____

_____

How are you similar to them?

_____

_____

_____

How are you different?

_____

_____

_____

What's your definition of a good friend, and how do you try to be one?

_____

_____

_____

Daughter Writes

Dear Mom,

Tell me about your closest friends when you were my age.

_____

_____

_____

What did you enjoy doing with them?

_____

_____

_____

How were you similar and different?

_____

_____

_____

Do you still keep in touch?

_____

_____

_____

What's your definition of a good friend, and how do you try to be one?

_____

_____

_____

Mom Writes

You and Me

Things we enjoy doing together

At home

In our community

Outside

With other people

We Write

Dear Mom,

Could you tell me about _____

_____

_____?

Mom Writes

Daughter, thank you for always

1 _____

2 _____

3 _____

I'm so grateful you never

Daughter Writes

Mom, thank you for always

1 _____
  _____

2 _____
  _____

3 _____
  _____

I'm so grateful you never

Dear Mom,

Tell me about a decision you made to make my life better, even though it was difficult for you.

Why did you do it?

How do you feel about that choice today?

Mom Writes

Dear Daughter,

Tell me about a difficult decision you recently had to make.

How did you ultimately choose what to do?

Why do you think it's important to examine hard situations or opportunities?

Mom Writes

The emojis I use most

The people or groups I message most

The last text I sent you, Daughter

The last photo
or meme I sent you

Daughter Writes

The emojis I use most

The people or groups I message most

The last text I sent you, Mom

The last photo
or meme I sent you

Dear Daughter,

On a scale of 1 to 5, how are you feeling about your changing body?

| 1 | 2 | 3 | 4 | 5 |

Tell me about it.

Dear Mom,

What are your thoughts on what I wrote?

Do you remember how you felt about your body when you were my age?

Mom Writes

Dear Daughter,

Do you feel like I trust you?

_____

_____

_____

_____

_____

_____

_____

_____

_____

Is there anything you wish I did differently?

_____

_____

_____

_____

_____

_____

_____

_____

_____

_____

Daughter Writes

Dear Mom,

What are your thoughts on what I just wrote?

_____
_____
_____
_____
_____
_____
_____
_____
_____
_____

Do you feel like you can trust me?

_____
_____
_____
_____
_____
_____
_____
_____
_____
_____
_____

Mom Writes

This is us
Food Edition

Our go-to snack

Daughter _____

Mom _____

Our beloved comfort food

Daughter

Mom

Our favorite pizza toppings

Daughter

Mom

Our eat-in-the-car, gotta-be-quick meal

Daughter _____

Mom _____

Our choice restaurant dinner

Daughter _____

Mom _____

Our guzzle-by-the-gallon beverage

Daughter _____

Mom _____

We Write

Our takes-all-day-to-cook pick for dinner

Daughter _____

Mom _____

Our fresh vegetable selections

Daughter _____

Mom _____

Our #1 carb

Daughter

Mom

Our hot summer day lunch

Daughter

Mom

Our I'm-so-cold, warm-me-up meal

Daughter _____

Mom _____

Our I-know-it's-strange, I-eat-it-anyway food

Daughter _____

Mom _____

Dear Mom,

How do you mend a broken heart?

Mom Writes

Dear Daughter,

Have you ever been so hurt or let down that your heart felt broken?
Tell me the story.

Mom Writes

Here's a keepsake from my life right now.

It's a

- ☐ ticket stub
- ☐ quote or poem
- ☐ receipt
- ☐ photo or picture
- ☐ wrapper
- ☐ school paper
- ☐ list or note
- ☐ _____

_____

I'm adding it to our journal because _____

_____

_____

_____

Daughter Writes

Here's a keepsake from my life right now.

It's a

☐ ticket stub   ☐ photo or picture   ☐ list or note

☐ quote or poem   ☐ wrapper   ☐ _____

☐ receipt   ☐ school paper   _____

I'm adding it to our journal because _____

_____

_____

_____

Mom Writes
This or That?

circle each preference →

Head	Heart
Go out	Stay in
See the future	Change the past
Time	Money
Watch the movie	Read the book
Unplugged	Online
Climate change is fact	Climate change is fake
The Rolling Stones	The Beatles
Comedy	Drama
The journey	The destination
Meme	GIF
Silence	Chatter
Halloween	Valentine's Day
Music	Podcast
Sci-fi	Rom-com
Mountains	Beach

Daughter Writes
This or That?

Head	Heart
Go out	Stay In
See the future	Change the past
Time	Money
Watch the movie	Read the book
Unplugged	Online
Climate change is fact	Climate change is fake
The Rolling Stones	The Beatles
Comedy	Drama
The journey	The destination
Meme	GIF
Silence	Chatter
Halloween	Valentine's Day
Music	Podcast
Sci-fi	Rom-com
Mountains	Beach

include any interesting asides!

Dear Mom,

Do you remember a moment when you felt really loved? Tell me about it.

Why does this memory matter to you?

Mom Writes

A typical dinner scene at our house

Daughter

Mom

We Write

Wonderful things we've done together

1 _____

2 _____

3 _____

4 _____

5 _____

6 _____

7 _____

8 _____

We Write

Interesting things we still need to do together

1 _____

2 _____

3 _____

4 _____

5 _____

6 _____

7 _____

8 _____

Daughter Writes

Mom, when you're frustrated with me, try to remember

_____

_____

_____

When I'm irritated with you, I'll try to remember

_____

_____

_____

Mom Writes

Daughter, when you're frustrated with me, try to remember

_____

_____

_____

When I'm irritated with you, I'll try to remember

_____

_____

_____

We Write

Dear Daughter,

I have a question for you: _____

_____

_____?

Daughter Writes

I always make time for

1

2

3

I never have time to

1

2

3

I enjoy time together to

1

2

3

Mom Writes

I always make time for

1

2

3

I never have time to

1

2

3

I enjoy time together to

1

2

3

Daughter Writes

I love celebrating this holiday: _____

It feels magical to me because _____

_____

I eat _____

I say _____

I see _____

I give _____

I wear _____

I feel _____

One of my favorite traditions is _____

_____

_____

I remember one time when _____

_____

_____

Daughter Writes

Mom Writes

I love celebrating this holiday: _____

It feels magical to me because _____

_____

I eat _____

I say _____

I see _____

I give _____

I wear _____

I feel _____

One of my favorite traditions is _____

_____

_____

I remember one time when _____

_____

_____

Dear Daughter,

What kind of technology do you use to communicate with your friends?

Record your current email
or username here.

How did you get that name?

My go-to device

What do you like about going online?

What do you dislike?

Do you ever feel pressured or uncomfortable about anything online?

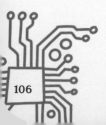

Daughter Writes

Dear Mom,

What kind of technology did you use to communicate with friends when you were my age?

Record your first email
address here. ➜

How did you get that address?

My original
go-to device

Did your parents ever take away your
technology privileges? Why?

What do you like about going online these days?

What do you dislike?

Mom Writes

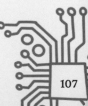

Daughter Writes

My typical weekday

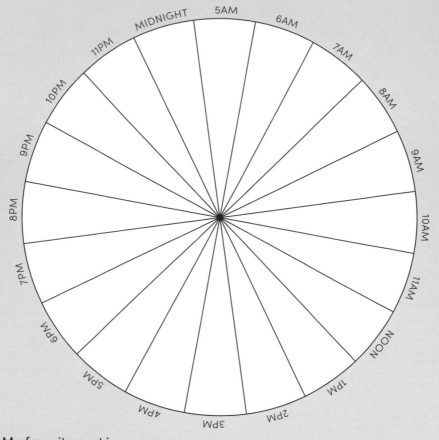

My favorite part is

_____

_____

I'm not really a fan of

_____

_____

Mom Writes
My typical weekday

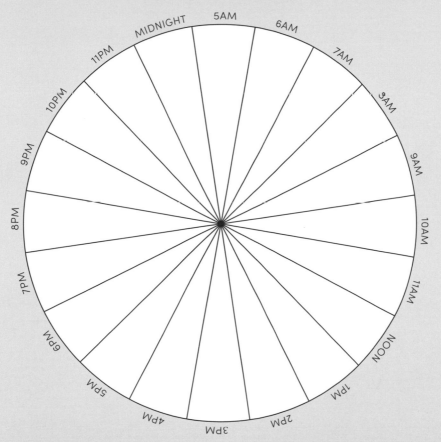

My favorite part is

_____

_____

I'm not really a fan of

_____

_____

Mom Writes

The money we have has enabled our family to

These are times when money doesn't matter to our family

I think it's important to set aside money for

To live within your means is to

I'm currently saving for

Debt is a problem when

I enjoy giving time or money to

Daughter Writes

Date

The money we have has enabled our family to

These are times when money doesn't matter to our family

I think it's important to set aside money for

To live within your means is to

I'm currently saving for

Debt is a problem when

I enjoy giving time or money to

Dear Mom,

Tell me about a relative I didn't know well.

Mom Writes

Currently on my

Desk

Daughter

Mom

Bed

Daughter

Mom

Bathroom sink

Daughter

Mom

Dear Mom,

What was one of your favorite jobs before I was born?

How old were you? And how much did you get paid?

What were your responsibilities?

Explain something interesting that you learned about yourself.

What made the job interesting and why did you stop?

Tell me about a mistake you made or lesson you learned.

Mom Writes

Dear Daughter,

What do you think about my favorite job?

Would you try it?

What kind of jobs would you like to try?

Tell me about the kind of work and life you dream of having when you're grown.

Dear Daughter,

Is there anything you've felt nervous to talk aloud with me about? Would you like to write it out here?

Daughter Writes

Dear Mom,

What are your thoughts on what I wrote?

Do you ever feel nervous to say something out loud? What do you do?

Dear Daughter,

If you could add, change, enforce, or eliminate one rule at our house, tell me about what you'd pick.

Daughter Writes

Dear Mom,

What do you think?

☐ Sure, let's try it

☐ I hadn't thought of that

☐ Sorry, we can't do that right now

☐ _____

because

Dear Daughter,

Design a new shirt for me.

Daughter Writes

Dear Mom,

Design a new shirt for me.

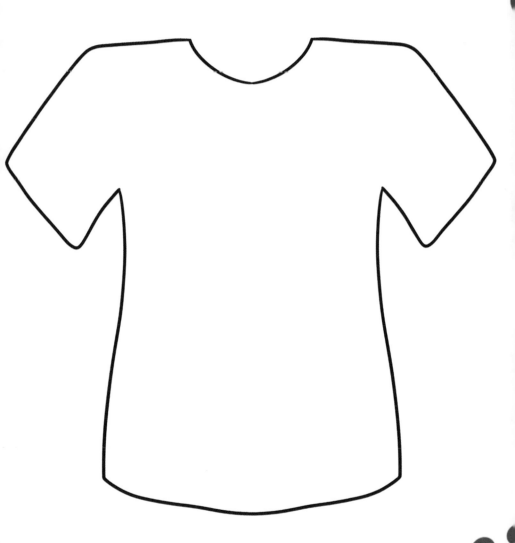

Daughter Writes

This or that?

circle each preference →

Sour cream	Guacamole
Summer	Winter
Video chat	Audio chat
Politically left	Politically right
Appetizer	Dessert
Half empty	Half full
Mini golf	Bowling
Gilmore Girls	Friends
Early	Late
Cotton candy	Corn dog
Science class	English class
Lennon	McCartney
Snow	Sand
Soup	Salad
Reality TV	Scripted TV
Roses	Tulips

Daughter Writes

Mom Writes
This or that?

Sour cream	Guacamole
Summer	Winter
Video chat	Audio chat
Politically left	Politically right
Appetizer	Dessert
Half empty	Half full
Mini golf	Bowling
Gilmore Girls	Friends
Early	Late
Cotton candy	Corn dog
Science class	English class
Lennon	McCartney
Snow	Sand
Soup	Salad
Reality TV	Scripted TV
Roses	Tulips

← include any interesting asides!

We love where we live in

因為

because

1 _____
_____

2 _____
_____

3 _____
_____

Shopping spot

Neighborhood

Food place

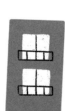

We Write

Around here, people:

So do we!

	Daughter	Mom
Eat	☐	☐
Drink	☐	☐
Say	☐	☐
Wear	☐	☐
Keep	☐	☐
Never	☐	☐
Always	☐	☐
Celebrate	☐	☐
Do this on weekends	☐	☐
Feel passionate about	☐	☐

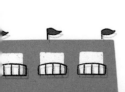

We Write

Around here, people can usually find us at:

Daughter _____

Mom _____

One area where we think our community could be improved is

One thing we'd never change is

We Write

Dear Daughter,

When you're grown, do you want to stay in our community or live somewhere else?

Where would you want to go?

Daughter Writes

Date

Dear Mom,

Is there anywhere else you'd like to live one day?

Mom Writes

Daughter Writes

Things we do differently

1 _____
_____

2 _____
_____

3 _____
_____

Things we do the same

1 _____
_____

2 _____
_____

3 _____
_____

Mom Writes

Things we do differently

1 _____
_____

2 _____
_____

3 _____
_____

Things we do the same

1 _____
_____

2 _____
_____

3 _____
_____

Daughter Writes

Mom, I have to admit that you were right about

Mom Writes

Daughter, I have to admit that you were right about

Dear Daughter,

What do you think about dating and relationships right now?

Do you have any questions for me?

Do you have anything you want to tell me?

Daughter Writes

Dear Mom,

What do you think about what I wrote?

Do you have any words of wisdom?

Mom Writes

Dear Daughter,

Tell me a story about a time when you worked really hard at something—
and succeeded! How did it make you feel?

Tell me a story about a time when you worked really hard and didn't
see the results you'd expected.

In hindsight, do you see any benefits to the outcome you experienced?

Mom Writes

Daughter, you deserve an award for

I'm proud to be your mom because

I still can't believe that you

One day, I hope you get the chance to

Know I'm always here for you because

To be beautiful means to be yourself.

–Thich Nhat Hanh

Dear Mom,

What are some of your favorite parts of motherhood?

Dear Daughter,

Do you ever find yourself feeling jealous of someone else? Tell me about a recent experience.

How do you feel about yourself when you're envious?

When you're not envying someone else, do you feel the same ways about yourself?

Daughter Writes

Dear Mom,

What do you think about what I told you?

Why do you think envy can be so difficult?

Would you tell me about a time when you felt jealous? What did you do about it?

Date

Dear Mom,

Do you vote? Why or why not?

What do you think makes a good candidate?

Mom Writes

Dear Daughter,

Do you think you'll vote? Why or why not?

What do you think makes a good candidate?

Dear Daughter,

What else would you like me to know?

Daughter Writes